Little Paws
And
Lion Hearts

Stories about
Pekingese dogs.

Written By
Leah Haney

PRINTED IN THE UNITED STATES
OF AMERICA
COPYRIGHT (2) 2014 LEAH HANEY
ISBN 13 9781497447851
ISBN 10 1497447852

Dedication

First and foremost, let me thank all of the ladies who submitted stories about their dogs.

This book is dedicated to my lovely little dog Mufin and all of the other Pekingese in rescue awaiting families of their own.

Several people helped me greatly. The writing of this book would not have come together so beautifully, without the help of Sally Jones, Nicki Taylor, and Sam Little .

MUFFIN

When I set out in search of my first dog there were two things I was absolutely sure of; I wanted a rescue dog and I wanted that dog to be a pug! A few weeks into my search my Aunt Trisha saw the wife of the man who ran a little, tiny shelter out in the woods of Summer, Maine. She told my Aunt they had recently taken in two pugs! As soon as my mother returned from work that night I dragged her right back into the truck and we took off for the shelter. I was quite surprised to be greeted by two smoosh-face, short legged, longhaired dogs.

"These aren't pugs." I said to the man who ran the shelter.

"Oh yeah they are," he replied. "They are just the long haired kind."

I knew better and I was disappointed, but they were still pretty cute so I decided to play with them while I was there anyway. I unlocked the kennel and dropped to my knees as I opened the door. Both the dogs came forward, but when I reached out for them, the male promptly jumped forward and bit me on the hand! I had barely had time to react when the little girl turned on him and chased him to the back of the kennel. She then strutted back to the front and right up into my lap, where she promptly flipped over for a belly rub. I looked at those big brown eyes and that teddy bear face and I was gone. This was my dog!

There was a bit of a problem though. The man who ran the shelter had taken a liking to my girl, as well, and was considering adopting her himself. So I decided to go back and show him how serious I was about this dog. On my fifth visit I took my father with me. While I snuggled the little girl in my lap I heard my Dad say to the shelter manager , "You will never get rid of my kid unless you give her this dog."

That little bit of man-to-man chat must have worked, because the shelter owner gave in! I signed the paperwork and that adorable little dog was mine. That is how I fell into the world of the Pekingese.

Though Muffin became immediately devoted to my mother and me, I could not help but notice that though Pekingese may share a similar face shape with pugs, there was none of the happy-go-lucky pug-type personality in this girl! Really, she was a bit on the grumpy side. She loved to play with other dogs but she had no problem snapping at the legs or faces of dogs three to four times her size if they seemed to question her place as the boss dog. She growled at strangers from the minute they arrived to the minute they left. She was happy to accompany me to the barn every morning for chores, but she had no fear of my horses and would climb right into their grain buckets at feeding time. She was incredibly stubborn about housebreaking. When she first came home I could keep her out in the yard for more than half an hour, yet she would sneak off and pee on my bedroom carpet five minutes after we came back inside!

It takes just a few minutes of internet research into the breed history of the Pekingese for explanation of all of Muffin's little quirks. It became clear it was written in her DNA. According to legend, a great lion fell in love with a Marmoset (a very tiny type of monkey). Knowing that they could never marry due to their great difference in size, the lion prayed to the patron saint of the animals to shrink him so he could be with his true love. The lion's wish was granted. The union of the couple resulted in what we now know as the Pekingese dog.

According to history, Pekingese were bred as companion

dogs and fashion accessories for the Chinese Emperors. The ancient breed standard, which can be found on the Pekingese Club of America's website actually makes reference to the different coat colors of the dogs matching the imperial robes.

"And for its color- let it be that a lion, a golden sable, to be carried in the sleeve of a yellow robe-or the color of a red bear, or a black and white bear-or stripped like a dragon-so that there may be dogs appropriate to every costume in the Imperial wardrobe."

Muffin

The smallest and most aggressive Pekes were carried in the sleeves of these robes to defend and scare off anyone threatening the royal they road with. Really, they were royal dogs themselves. Normal townspeople were actually expected to bow when one walked down the street! The punishment for stealing one of the special dogs was death!

Half lion, half monkey, ancient Chinese royalty, a hidden personal defense system. Of course this dog was brave, stubborn, smart and a little stuck on herself. She certainly came by her giant personality honestly.

I began working with Little Paws Big Hearts Pekingese Rescue in the summer of 2013. Emergency pulls or dogs in need of immediate medical attention can come to my home for a few days and the necessary treatments before going to one of the rescue's regular foster homes. (We are only a temporary stop because Muffin says she'll tolerate a visit but only one Pekingese can live in this house at a time). Hurricane and Paris, the two dogs that have come to stay with us, have had the same funny and independent attitude that my Muffin has. That really got me thinking, these are not your average little dogs. They do not need to be dressed in sweaters and carried in a purse. They have a truly unique and larger-then-life personality. There must be a great number of fun stories about exploits. So I set out to collect them. Facebook was a handy tool. Some of these stories came from friends who responded to my probably excessive posting about Muffin and Pekingese rescue with "Hey I used to have a Pekingese," but most came from people on the rescue's Facebook page.

I think they give an accurate peek into this fabulous breed of dog!

Breed History Sources
The American Kennel Club
The Pekingese Club of America
dogs 101

Dude

Being short on sight doesn't stop a Pekingese

Susan Gayle is the co-director of Little Paws Big Hearts Pekingese Rescue in Maine. She is well versed in the personality quirks of the breed. Her story revolves around Pekingese bravery she witnessed in two rescued boys who entered into her home for foster but ended up staying.

The first boy Frankie, a handsome red Peke that came from Illinois. He still had stitches from the removal of one eye and was almost blind in the other, but he became Susan's love from the moment his little paws set foot in her house, so she adopted him herself.

The second Peke is Dude a mellow mannered all white boy who came to Maine by way of California. He also had had an eye removed before he came to stay with Susan. As Susan began to take Dude to rescue events in an effort to find him a home, she could not help but notice that he was an absolute rock star. He loved going out and meeting people. None of her other dogs really cared for these events so Dude stayed with Susan to be the rescue's front man!

Susan says these two boys become one on walks around their neighborhood. Dude becomes Frankie's eyes so to speak. They lean tightly on each other while walking down the sidewalk. It's quite apparent that Dude knows that Frankie needs a little extra looking after. One evening when Susan's husband Mike took the boys for their evening jaunt around their cul-de-sac, Dude showed them just how seriously he took that task.

One home along their route had a couple of big, black dogs with questionable intentions towards little dogs. They were always shut in on a porch attached to the house, so they did not seem to be much to worry about. On this particular night, however, something went wrong. When one of the dogs jumped up on the porch door to bark at Mike and the boys the door popped open! The dog came running across its yard, jumped a gate at the end of the driveway and charged across the street straight for the two little Pekingese!

Dude was not about to let his blind friend be pushed around by this black bully. He charged straight out to the end of his leash and met the bigger aggressor head on! The big dog was so surprised to be met with no fear that he stopped in his tracks! He had to slink back to his own yard, bestead in intimidation by a little white Pekingese protecting his friend!

Age is nothing but a number to a Pekingese

Lisa Swager got her love of Pekingese from her parents. At one point her parents had ten rescued Pekes at their home in Butler, Pennsylvania. One pair of girls particularly sticks out in her memory. Buttons and Bows were a fawn colored pair of elderly sisters. Their owner had fallen ill and been placed in a nursing home. The girls spent five months living alone in their owner's home with a neighbor coming in to feed them daily until Lisa's parents took them in.

One day while the Pekes were out enjoying some time in the backyard a hound dog Lisa assumed had strayed away from a hunting party wandered up to the fence. Now all the Pekes were sounding the alarm, but Buttons and Bows were ready for a fight! These old ladies held their ground on the inside of the fence, roaring like little miniature lionesses protecting their pride. Lisa could not even call them inside for laughing at the ferocity of these two senior citizens threating the trespasser.

The hound dog, however, did not find fear in Buttons' and Bows' threats. He used his nose to pop up the bottom of the fence and came trotting right in!

At this point Lisa decided the girls had had enough of their fun and scooped them up and into the house. The hound was wearing tags, and the owner was called to come collect him. Turns out he hadn't strayed from a hunt, he had just plain strayed.

Buttons and Bows were in their glory that afternoon. they had a prouder than usual Pekingese strut. The intruder was gone and it had to have been their superb guard dog skills that chased him away.

Spanky and Obi

Pekingese puppy finds an interesting friend.

Ali M of Florida likes to call her place the Zoo because of the array of animals living there. Her little Pekingese puppy Obi, loved being the youngest member of the pack, because, as you know the baby gets the majority of the attention. He was going to have to learn to share though because Ali was a rescuer at heart and there was always a four-legged friend in need of a loving home.

Spanky was brought into Ali's place of work to be euthanized for a badly mangled leg. You see rodents are shipped to pet stores in boxes and poor Spanky had been accidently stapled to the box when it was closed up for shipment. Yup, that's right, rodents, poor injured Spanky was a rat. Ali's veterinarian did not want to euthanize Spanky and choose to amputate the leg instead. After surgery Spanky went home with Ali.

Now Ali's older animals had become quite accustomed to new animals moving in. Her German Shepherd, Dachshund, Jack Russell, rabbit, and cats had little interest in the new three level cage that held the newest member of the family. The little Pekingese puppy however was extremely interested in Spanky.

Obi started bringing all his toys and his meals over to the cage. He even took to sleeping near the cage to be close to the little rat at night. At first Spanky stayed as far away from Obi as possible, but the little Peke persisted in hanging around. Spanky became less and less nervous of the dog and could be found lying closer and closer to where the curious dog sniffed at the cage.

Spanky had been living with the family for a month when Ali heard the Peke's play bark coming from the rat's room, that sort of raspy/gurgling/chirpy noise that a little smooshed face makes when it gets really excited. When Ali went in to investigate, she could not believe her eyes. Obi was running back and forth play bowing in front of the rats cage and Spanky was right there to meet him!! The little rat was actually leaping up in the air and shaking his body in excitement. So Ali decided it was time to let Spanky out of his cage. She put him on the floor and was amazed to see him run straight to the little Peke puppy and start grooming him!

From then on Spanky's cage door was hardly ever closed, and the rat and Pekingese were inseparable. They would be found chasing each other around the room and wrestling. Many times the Pekingese and the rat would even curl up together for afternoon naps. Spanky even

16

taught Obi how to climb up on the bed! Most people would find it pretty strange that a dog and a rat would end up being best friends, but Ali wasn't because in her zoo anything was possible..

Murphy and Coco

A Pekingese heals a broken heart

The Monahan family of Illinois loves dogs. They were heartbroken when they lost their seventeen year old Pomeranian, Bailey. Even their little Japanese Chin, Coco, became despondent and took to sleeping most of the day. Mrs. Monahan decided they needed to find Coco another friend and began to search for another Pomeranian on Pet Finder. She fell for Gabby, a little Pomeranian/Pekingese mix, available for adoption through Little Big Hearts Pekingese Rescue.

Unfortunately, little Gabby became ill not long after adoption. She was diagnosed with Viral Encephalitis (inflammation of the brain) and passed away just a short five weeks after coming to live with the Monahan's. The family was devastated to have lost a second dog in such a short time. They would not go through this heartbreak again.

"No way, no how, no dogs are entering the Monahan household," Mr. Monahan huffed through his grieving tears.

Susan the director of Little Paws, and Kelly, the rescue's local volunteer, were not ready to accept that however. They checked in with the Monahan's regularly, recommending a particular dog here and there that they thought might fit well in their home, but Mr. Monahan and Coco continued to say no. Kelly even brought a lovely male over to meet them, but Cocoa lashed out at him so feverishly that she was foaming at the mouth. It seemed the family was going to stand on no more dogs. However, Mrs. Monahan still wasn't ready to give up on the idea.

Kelly called Mrs. Monahan one beautiful September morning.

"I think I have the one," she told her. "Coco is going to love him. I just know it"

The ladies planned a secret rendezvous in the local park. When Mrs. Monahan met the adorable cream-colored male named Murphy, she knew everything was going to work out. Coco and Murphy exchanged a calm greeting and settled down into the grass side by side to relax. This brought forth the big decision of whether to take Murphy home to meet Mr. Monahan or not.

I hope this doesn't send me to divorce court Mrs. Monahan thought as she made arrangements with Kelly to bring Murphy to the house, but with Coco having been won over so easily she decided it was worth the risk!

She and Kelly burst in with the dogs in ambush style.

To her surprise there was not a word of argument at their arrival. When Mr. Monahan laid eyes on sweet Murphy it was like a young boy had been reunited with his long lost childhood dog. He sat on the floor playing with Murphy for a while and then looked up at Kelly with big eyes and asked "Can we keep him for the weekend?"

Well the weekend came and went and Murphy never left. He and Mr. Monahan are attached at the hip. If his Dad isn't home Murphy spends his time curled up with Coco. Poor Mrs. Monahan feels like a bit of an outsider sometimes, after all, it was her idea and hard work that brought Murphy home in the first place!

Murphy and Dad

A Pekingese does not consider
Itself a little dog.

Trisha Haney purchased a little white female Pekingese puppy from a friend in Limerick, Maine for seventy five dollars. She named her Flora. They became immediate friends and Flora was always by Trisha's side. Flora sat at the table while Trisha ate dinner, watched from the doorway while Trisha brushed her teeth; Flora even let Trisha brush hers from time to time, as well. Flora's favorite pastime, though, was to sit next to Trisha on the couch while she painted her fingernails, and present her own paws for a manicure, as well.

Flora grew up to consider herself Trisha's personal guard dog. If anyone raised their voice to Trisha, Flora would chase after them. However, if Trisha raised her voice to someone else, Flora would chase after that person too! One day the gas station attendant started to reach into the car trying to pet Flora.

"I wouldn't do that ," Trisha warned him.

"Why not? He asked, " She's just a little dog. What harm could she do?"

He leaned into the driver's side window and that little white Peke went after him like a coyote after a rabbit. He jumped back with such a look of surprise that Trisha could not help but laugh, she had warned him.

Flora wagged her tail and grinned up at Trisha proudly. She's shown that man just how big Pekingese could be!

A Peke loves to be in the thick of the adventure!

Suki and Tasha

Laura Lowell had two great dogs growing up, Tasha, a red Irish Setter and Suki, a fawn Pekingese. Now Laura loved her dogs but she had been dreaming of a horse for as long as she could remember. When she was sixteen, she realized that maybe she didn't need a horse for all the things she wanted to do. So Laura purchased a dog harness for Tasha to see if she would pull Laura's red sled through the snow!

Pull she did. Tasha was more than happy to tow the sled

wherever Laura wanted to go. Suki, the Pekingese was not about to be left out of any adventures. Anywhere Laura and Tasha went in that sled, the little Peke was right there in the front of it, pulling on a bit of rope or barking encouragement to the setter, racing ahead of them. Sometimes when Suki got really excited, she would jump out and run alongside of the sled. Those little bowed Peke legs could not keep pace with that long setter's stride for long, but no worries, Suki would simply hop back into the sled to ride some more.

Sixteen year old Laura traveled many miles of snowmobile trails around her hometown of Rumford Center, Maine in this fabulously unique fashion, snuggled with a Pekingese in a little red sled pulled by a loping Irish Setter!

Percy

A Pekingese may retain that ancient guard dog philosophy

Vicki D. of Tennessee had owned golden retrievers most of her life. After the last one passed to the rainbow bridge, she decided that due to her rheumatoid arthritis she needed to move to a smaller dog the next time. She remembered that as a little girl, that the lady next door had always had Pekingese. Vicki had always been interested in them but her mother was very allergic so they could never have one. But there was nothing to stop her now.!

She fell in love with an adorable cinnamon-colored boy with a black muzzle she located on petfinder.com. His name was Percy. Little Paws Big Hearts Pekingese Rescue had pulled him from a West Virginia shelter where he had been housed after being abandoned in a local dog park. He was in pretty bad shape, severely malnourished and anemic from being overrun with worms and fleas. The rescue took care of the bugs and got him on the road to better health. Vicki and her husband drove up from Tennessee to get him.

Percy may have been much smaller than a Golden Retriever, but he turned out to be twice the handful! His training had gone super well, so Vicki had begun to take him out into the yard without a leash. Percy had been coming right back inside after his business was done and Vicki always went out with him, so she was not worried about him running off. Imagine her surprise when one afternoon Percy spotted the neighbor's black Labrador, Maddie, out with her owner and he shot across the yard and went after her! Luckily Maddie is a lover not a fighter, and her owner was able to keep the dogs separated until

Vicki could come scoop Percy up!

"You just lost your leash privileges permanently little man" she scolded him as they went back into the house!

The next incident came at the vet clinic while Percy was on his leash. They were sitting in the lobby waiting for their appointment when another customer came in with a rescued racing Greyhound. Percy took one look at that dog and charged. When his leash stopped him, Vicki says he dropped and spun like the alligator death roll until he popped his collar right off so he could go after the bigger dog! Percy lucked out again, although Greyhounds were bred to hunt small, furry creatures, this one took Percy's big attitude in stride and nobody was hurt.

"I thought keeping you on the leash was enough to keep you out of trouble" Vicki scolded him again a little exasperated at his behavior. Now Percy's feet are never allowed to touch the floor when visiting the vet!

Percy's fighting spirit may have caused them a problem or two, but it has also come in handy.

One morning Vicki and Percy stopped to fill the car up with gas. When they finished, Vicki got back into her car, and as she turned to attach her seat belt, a woman leaned in through the window and tried to steal her money. Well, that little, adorable, cinnamon Peke blew up like a Tasmanian devil and flew across the car, jumping at the woman's face like he'd be happy to take a snip right off the end of her nose!

The would be thief jumped back hollering. "That dog tried to bite me!" Percy continued to raise a ruckus in the car right back at her. Vicki took advantage of the chaos to drive across the street to call the police.

Though Percy is a little warrior when he feels it's called for he is also a gentle soul. There are a couple of cats in their family. The calico cat is named Tulip, who really runs the house. Whatever bed, blanket, or chair Percy tries to sleep in Tulip comes along and nudges and pesters him until he has to get up. Percy never fights back, he never even lifts a lip to her, just moves off quietly to the next available place to settle in for a nap! Tulip can even push him out of Vicki's lap! The sweet boy just gives a disgruntled snort and goes down to the floor where he can curl up on his Momma's feet instead! A Pekingese is always full of surprises.

Kim and Muffin

Sometimes food is the key to Pekingese Cooperation

Kim Cushman grew up in Vermont, and the family pet was a beautiful, blonde and white Pekingese named Muffin. Kim remembers with great fondness what she always considered the slightly odd sight of her very tall and manly father walking the fluffy and very tiny Muffin on the end of the leash. Her pretty looks were not the fanciest thing about Muffin however, her claim to fame was her variety of tricks!

Muffin knew all the regulars: "Shake, rollover," and "sit pretty," but she also had some big numbers! Her best was "scratch my back." Kim would lay on the floor on her side and Muffin would lay on her side behind her like they were spooning and she would scratch with her front paws. Then Kim would say "switch sides," Muffin would hop over her and start the process all over again! The little dog would work at this trick until she wore herself out and had to stop because she was panting like crazy!

Now Pekingese are known for being extremely independent and doing things only as they please. So why was this precious, blond Peke so happy to put on a big production of tricks for her family? They had a secret weapon. Little Muffin would do anything for the overwhelming power of cheese!

Sometimes food is also the key to winning over a Peke's heart!

When Jamie Duff was twelve years old, her older sister got a job waitressing at the local Friendly's restaurant in Dalton, Massachusetts. The manager mentioned to her that he had a dog that his children were no longer taking care of and he wanted to get rid of it. Jamie's family members were big animal lovers so her sister told her father about the dog that night. He agreed to take the dog right away without even knowing what the dog was. He met the manager at the restaurant and picked up what turned out to be a little, red one-eyed Pekingese. They named him Champ.

Things did not go super smoothly with Champ's adoption. At first he was lethargic and vomited his food often. Jamie's mother cooked him a large batch of beef stew and fed him small frequent meals. With this care and patience, his belly was restored to better health. However, that brought forth a second issue. Every time twelve year old Jamie went near little Champ, he would snarl and look like he would like nothing better than to attack her. Her father turned this into an even bigger problem for young Jamie when he announced to the family a new house rule.

"No one in this house is allowed to feed Champ except Jamie. Every bite of food he gets has to come from her hands."

Jamie was not impressed. Champ obviously hated her and she was definitely afraid of him, but she did as her father instructed. She brought him his breakfast and supper and even gave him a couple of treats every day. It took about two weeks, but Champ began to look for Jamie when it was time to eat and they finally became comfortable with each other.

Two months later, the restaurant manager called to say his kids missed the dog and asked for him back. Jamie's father told him no way. Champ had become a well-established member of the Duff family.

Champ marched to the beat of his own drummer. Hooked to a leash he refused to take a step, however, left free he would follow at the family's heels wherever they went. He would sit up all through dinner waiting for his turn. He always got something when they finished, because after all, people food had played a fairly important role in bringing him back to good health. His favorite treat were eggs. He would come running from any area of the house at the crack of an eggshell.

Champ never seemed to forget that Jamie's father was the one who had taken him from that non-caring home. When Mr. Duff was home, the girls really did not exist to the little Peke. He stayed right next to their father every minute. That didn't matter though. He had still won Jamie's heart. He lived with the Duff family for around thirteen years to the estimated age of eighteen years old. Jamie has had six other fabulous Pekes since then and is forever thankful for the stubborn, little, one-eyed red Champ who introduced her to her favorite breed-even if it was with a growl.

Muffin and Leah

The surprising power of my Pekingese

Due to my growing experience with Pekingese, I now believe that Muffin saw me coming. Stubborn pride can spot stubborn pride form a mile away! She knew I was the one who would keep coming back until the man at the shelter would let me take her home. Muffin turned out to have some pretty severe problems with allergies. At certain points in her life there has been minimal hair on her body due to constant chewing and scratching at her skin. More than once there were suggestions that I put her to sleep. I just couldn't do it. She was so darn tough. As long as she was willing to fight, so was I. It took seven long years to find the right combination of treatments to manage her severe itch, but we did. The right diet, frequent bathing, and all perfume-free soaps and cleaners in our house and my fourteen year old girl is now comfortable in her own skin.

I have read certain articles that state due to a Peke's extreme stubbornness and difficulty to train, they are not very intelligent. I totally disagree. Muffin is the most clear and effective canine communicator I have ever met. When I come home before dinner I am greeted by an excited dancing dog with a wagging tail. If I come home after dinner I am greeted by a chorus of angry barks from the minute I come through door until the moment her dish full of dog food hits the floor! I am lucky enough to be allowed to bring my dogs to work with me when I have the mind to-or more like when Muffin has the mind to come! Most times when she accompanies me it is because she goes out after breakfast, sits down next to my driver's side door and refuses to come back in. My Pekingese will always tell me exactly what she wants! No interpretation necessary!

This small little girl has blessed me in so many ways. In the midst of searching for the best way to take care of Muffin's allergy problems I accepted a job working for the local veterinary clinic with the hope of an employee discount. That job turned into a full-blown career. A client from that vet clinic set me up on a blind date with the man who would be my husband.

One of my major dreams since high school was to become an author of a book. I have published several articles in newspapers but have never managed to capture the inspiration to complete a large project until now. Muffin has made me such a fan of this breed that I wanted to share my love for them with the world. My life is a bit of the six degrees of separation from my Pekingese!

Pekingese Rescue

Several of these stories were collected from ladies who are members of the Little Paws Big Hearts Pekingese Rescue Facebook page. The rescue was started by two women, one from Maine and one from Virginia. They met through a Pekingese fan page of Facebook. These ladies work tirelessly to take Pekes out of hard situations and place them into loving homes. They started the rescue in June of 2011 and have placed seven-five dogs in a short three years. Some dogs are owner surrenders, but many come from high kill shelters in the south. The rescue founders also keep watch over (free for the taking) ads on Craigslist and offer to take the dogs into rescue to ensure they get vetted and placed in approved homes.

Most of the dogs come in needing vet care. That could

simply be vaccinations, or it could be major anesthetic procedures like dental extractions or removal of an ulcerated eye. The organization's bills are endless. Compounding this, due to the strong-minded nature of the breed, many Pekes remain in rescue for a long time before the perfect home with an understanding of Pekingese personality can be found.

I experienced this first hand when I was asked to temporarily take in Paris, an older female Peke with an extremely bad eye infection. She had been turned in to a local shelter where they were having a very difficult time handling her and treating her eyes as she was very aggressive due to her discomfort. The shelter asked L.P.B.H.P.R. to step in and take over her care.

Paris spent one week with me for her initial treatment then moved into one of the rescue's regular foster homes. Unfortunately she could not settle in the home and that quickly escalated toward the people, as well! Her behavior became so aggressive the foster family could not keep her anymore. Susan Plante Gayle the co-director of Little Paws Pekingese Rescue and I began searching for a dog-free foster home for her, not something easy to find.

Luckily, Wendy, a co-worker who had met Paris while she was in my care, stepped up and offered to keep Paris temporarily. Wendy did have one other dog and there were some issues in the beginning. At first, Wendy was unsure that she would be able to keep Paris for long. However, Wendy was patient and she took the time to learn Paris' triggers and what bothered her. After about four and a half months they knew each other's routines so well, Wendy began to be unable to picture life without her!

Paris is a bit of a naughty dog, and like most Pekes, wants to do things in her own time and on her own terms. Wendy tells stories of her refusing to come inside in freezing cold temperatures because she's too busy searching the bushes for chipmunks. When Wendy is calling her, Paris will simply turn an ear back to show she can hear her then Paris will scoot further out into the yard! Wendy does not tell stories with irritation but with giggles and affection in her voice. That is the power of the Pekingese.

Paris spent eight months bouncing around in rescue before she found her perfect home with Wendy. Her mini saga is just a small example of the extensive work the ladies of the rescue do regularly to help these dogs. Her medical care (vaccinations and treating her eyes and allergies) is also just a small example of the associated costs. It is my greatest hope that this book will benefit L.P.B.H.P.R's efforts in some way. Please join their Facebook group or go to their website. www.littlepawsbigheartspekerescue.webs.com where they have many fundraising items for sale in their web store. Please peruse their photo gallery of dogs needing home and consider adopting. Be warned this breed is bold, brazen, smart and can be oh so naughty.

They will challenge you in many ways, but once a Pekingese takes hold of your heart, it will own it forever!

Paris and Wendy

About the Author

Animals and writing are Leah's passion. She began her writing career with canine healthcare articles and breed profiles for a Maine publication called the Down East Dog News. Leah lives with her husband, dogs and horses in the same western Maine Mountains where she was born and raised.

Leah and Muffin

Made in the USA
Lexington, KY
23 June 2014